How to use this workbook

Structure

The activities in this workbook will help you develop the skills and knowledge that you will need to achieve your best grade in A-level English Literature, whichever exam board specification you are following.

Each section offers a clear structure with activities that gradually increase in difficulty:

- **Starting out:** accessible activities that offer an introduction to the topic.
- **Developing your ideas:** skills-building activities that look in more detail at particular aspects of the text.
- **Taking it further:** more challenging tasks that will test your understanding of the text and consolidate your learning.

Boosting your skills

The final chapter of the workbook offers exam-focused activities that allow you to apply the skills you have developed. It also includes step-by-step guidance on the Assessment Objectives, and how to cover them in your written responses.

Features

Key terms

Definitions of key concepts and terminology. Understanding these and using them correctly in your written responses will help gain marks for AO1.

Key skills

Concise explanations of important skills to develop during your A-level studies. A variety of skills are covered, from fundamental ones such as analysing the structure of a text or embedding quotations in your writing, up to more advanced skills that are necessary to gain the top grades, such as exploring different interpretations of characters.

Challenge yourself

Advanced tasks that will push you further and help prepare you to achieve your best grade in the exams. They often focus on context (AO3), connections between texts (AO4) or critical interpretations of them (AO5).

Answers can be found at: www.hoddereducation.co.uk/workbookanswers

Introduction

Skirrid Hill, Owen Sheers' second collection of poetry, was published in 2005 to critical acclaim. A promising young writer who had previously impressed critics and readers alike with his debut poetry collection, *The Blue Book,* Sheers writes in a number of forms other than poetry, including novels, plays and non-fiction. He draws heavily on his childhood in Wales and on key Welsh poets, but his work is often seen as more accessible and down to earth, using free verse and a clear didactic style. Indeed, this last aspect is one that has received some criticism, with particular lines from *Skirrid Hill* being singled out as being too obvious and lacking nuance or ambiguity by reviewers like Sarah Crown in the *Guardian.*

Sheers returns to many of the themes and indeed locations of his first collection in *Skirrid Hill.* Born in Fiji, with Welsh heritage and an English university education, he explores his own identity, and often links this to considerations of masculinity in modern life. Conflict and conflicting emotions and times are one of the ways in which he examines these ideas. Many of the poems are about love, too, often focused on particular pivotal moments in relationships. The collection can be seen in two halves: the first more personal and intimate, looking back through history and in particular at national and family history; the second looking forward and outward and more widely at the modern world.

Studying *Skirrid Hill* at AS/A-level and using this workbook

Your studies of poetry at GCSE will be useful as you tackle this set text for A-level. It is still important to be able to identify and comment on the use of language terms and poetic devices, but you also need to consider bigger ideas such as rhyme and rhythm, voice and tone, typicality and links between poems inside and outside the collection. It is important to view the text as a collection, and not simply as a group of poems. The way that Sheers has arranged the poems, placing some side by side and some with similar ideas or themes further apart, is all part of his crafting of the text. This book follows the order of the poems in *Skirrid Hill* to help you chart the shifts and changes, considering the patterning of the original.

Throughout the book, there are key terms that you should try to incorporate into your own critical vocabulary. As you encounter new terminology, write down definitions and examples to help you learn the idea and correct spelling: flashcards can be very good for this. Being able to write well about the poems is as important at A-level as knowing the poems, so take time to follow links to critical articles as a way of deepening your understanding of how critics write. Choose quotations with care, and don't be afraid to rewrite longer answers when you revise, editing your earlier ideas as your knowledge of the text and your examination board's requirements becomes clearer.

A solid understanding of literary, social, historical and cultural references will help you make sense of Sheers' points of view and inspiration: use the **Challenge yourself** sections to read widely around your text, too. Sheers draws on a number of other poets and traditions in this collection, including R.S. Thomas, Seamus Heaney, the Romantics and T.S. Eliot, and it is worth spending some time familiarising yourself with these poets, as well as contemporaries like Carol Ann Duffy, to further your understanding of Sheers' work.

You do not need to tackle every activity in this book or to know every poem in equal detail: select the poems that are most appropriate for your particular examination board and style of questions, and ensure you know them in great depth, and then visit the remaining poems more briefly. Key poems are indicated with an asterisk (*) next to the title. If you are studying this text for comparison in the examination with another text such as the poems of Seamus Heaney or a modern novel, make notes on key themes and ideas in the other text as you revise these poems, making brief, regular links to consolidate your understanding of both texts as you work through this book.

Epigraph and title

1   What does the title 'Skirrid Hill' suggest to you?

    ....

    ....

    ....

Skirrid: From the Welsh *Ysgrid*. A derivation of *Ysgariad*, meaning divorce or separation.

2   What 'separations' can you think of, in life, literature and love? On a separate piece of paper, create a concept map of your initial ideas.

3   Why might a collection of poetry have an **epigraph**?

    ....

    ....

    ....

    ....

Epigraph: A short quotation at the beginning of a poem, novel or chapter, which suggests a theme or idea.

4   What is suggested by the *Skirrid Hill*'s epigraph, the T.S. Eliot poem 'East Coker'?

    ....

    ....

    ....

5   Which of your other set texts has an epigraph? Are they used in ways that are similar to or different from the ways in which Sheers uses Eliot?

    ....

    ....

    ....

Poems

'Last Act'*

STARTING OUT

1. To whom might the poem be addressed?

   ....

   ....

2. What do you think is meant by the lines 'Because / isn't this always the last act?'

   ....

   ....

   ....

3. On a copy of the poem, highlight each of the following categories in a different colour:

   - Semantic field of (words related to) performance or culture
   - Interesting verbs
   - Pronouns

DEVELOPING YOUR IDEAS

4. What do each of the following images suggest? Try to think of two different interpretations for each.

   (a) 'missing teeth'

   ....

   ....

   ....

   ....

   (b) 'stuck record'

   ....

   ....

   ....

   ....

CONTINUED ➡

Answers can be found at: www.hoddereducation.co.uk/workbookanswers

(c) 'countdown'

....

....

....

(d) 'bowing'

....

....

....

....

TAKING IT FURTHER

5   Circle the view that fits more closely with your own ideas and explain your choice in the space below.

- 'Last Act' is more a confession than a celebratory invocation to the muse.

- 'Last Act' is impersonal and merely functions as a way to establish the inherent universality and lack of personal or intimate revelations in the collection.

....

....

....

....

....

....

....

....

Invocation to the muse: An address to one of the Greek goddesses of culture, daughters of the goddess of memory, who were traditionally thanked for inspiring the work of art that followed. It's the origin of our English word 'museum' – the house of the muses.

'Mametz Wood'*

STARTING OUT

1   Use revision or history websites to research the First World War battle of Mametz Wood that inspired this poem, then complete the paragraph below.

> The battle took place as part of the First World War between the dates of .... and
> ...., and formed part of the battle of the ....
> The main regiment involved on the Allied side was the ....,
> including the .... division and the 14th .... Around
> .... men died or were wounded on the Allied side.

2   Match the word to the definition to make sure you understand the language of the poem.

CHIT	A mythical dance of death often found in medieval art
RELIC	An object that should not be there, often used as a medical term
SENTINEL	A religious artefact
FOREIGN BODY	A small piece of paper
MOSAIC	Artwork or floor covering made up of tiny fragments of stone
DANCE-MACABRE	To dig up or discover
UNEARTHING	A watchman; to guard

DEVELOPING YOUR IDEAS

3   Sound is used in the poem to emphasise different feelings in each stanza:

- to evoke feelings of both peace and sadness
- to emphasise ideas of destruction and fragmentation
- to build a sense of apprehension and tension
- to evoke a sense of mourning

Match the suggested effect to the technique or replace with your own ideas, and use short quotations from the poem to justify your analysis.

(a) The first stanza uses sibilance ...

....

....

....

Sibilance: The use of s or z sounds; often indicates soft or sinister effects.

CONTINUED

Answers can be found at: www.hoddereducation.co.uk/workbookanswers

(b) The second stanza uses sharp plosive sounds ...

....

....

....

(c) The third stanza uses long vowel sounds ...

....

....

....

(d) The final stanza uses sibilance ...

....

....

....

Plosive: Denoting a particular kind of consonant sound – such as d, p or b – where air is stopped and then released, in a kind of spitting out. It can sound abrupt or aggressive.

TAKING IT FURTHER

4   The first half of the poem uses far more similes and metaphors to describe the pieces of bone as they are discovered, whereas the second half is more blunt and literal. Why do you think Sheers has made this choice?

....

....

....

5   The fragments are described at first in ascending order of size and importance, until the final image, which is less substantial. Why do you think Sheers has made this choice? Make notes on each fragment below, considering what situations and connotations are suggested by each.

(a) 'chit'

....

....

CONTINUED ➡

(b) 'china plate'

....

....

(c) 'relic'

....

....

(d) 'broken bird's egg'

....

....

Challenge yourself

Listen to or read Sheers' own description of why he wrote the poem at the Poetry Archive website. What does this add to your understanding of the poem and Sheers' own motivation for writing?

'The Farrier'*

STARTING OUT

1 Make two lists of imagery used in the poem: one of stereotypically masculine imagery; one of stereotypically feminine imagery.

....	....
....	....
....	....
....	....
....	....
....	....
....	....

2 Which gender is the dominant motif? Write a sentence justifying your choice.

....

....

CONTINUED ➔

3   Match the terms to the definition.

FLANK	Someone who makes and attaches horseshoes to horses
FETLOCK	Joint in a horse's leg
BAY	Soft part under a horse's foot
FARRIER	Horse's side
FROG	Brown horse

DEVELOPING YOUR IDEAS

4   Sheers focuses entirely on the farrier's job, treating him as an archetype. Which word emphasises this? What part of speech is this?

....

Archetype: Representative or typical example of something, such as a specific type of character in a play or from society.

5   The poem is a vigenette, that gives clues about the farrier's character. What might be revealed about his personal interests, daily life, qualities or behaviour by the following quotations?

Vignette: Brief sketch or episode from daily life evoking feelings and ideas.

(a) 'Blessing himself'

....

....

....

(b) 'waits'

....

....

....

(c) 'careful not to look her in the eye'

....

....

....

(d) 'gritted between his teeth'

....

....

....

CONTINUED ➡

(e) 'a seamstress pinning the dress of the bride'

....

....

....

(f) 'gives her a slap'

....

....

....

6   Decide which words or phrases in the poem are being discussed in the comments below, and which interpretations you find more convincing.

(a) An unexpected colloquialism is used, which either relieves tension in the poem and suggests a crude and masculine kind of humour, or alternatively is very demeaning to the horse.

....

....

(b) This verb suggests either a cold and scientific attitude, or that there is treasure to be revealed.

....

....

TAKING IT FURTHER

7   Some stanzas are **enjambed** and some begin new sentences. Annotate your text in two colours to signal which is which. Why might Sheers have done this?

....

....

....

....

....

Enjambed: Where an idea or clause continues over the end of a line and onto the next. It is the opposite of being end-stopped.

CONTINUED ➡

8 (a) Fill in the Venn diagram below by writing romantic and sexual imagery in the circle on the left, violent imagery in the circle on the right and images that are both romantic, sexual and violent in the centre.

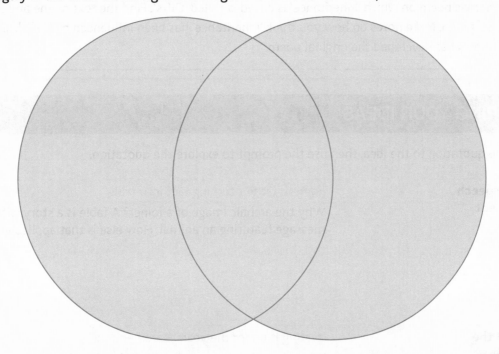

(b) How do these images in the centre of the diagram contribute to the overall effect?

....

Challenge yourself

Listen to Sheers reading the poem on the Poetry Archive website. Annotate a copy of the poem to show where he pauses (use '/' or '...') and where he uses emphasis (underline those words). Next to each annotation, write an adjective to describe the feeling and tone at that moment, such as 'nostalgic' or 'aggressive'.

'Inheritance'*

STARTING OUT

'Inheritance' is a dialectical poem about the traits that Sheers has inherited from each parent. The first two stanzas are heptets, and the last stanza is a sestet.

Dialectical: A method of reasoning that uses two different viewpoints to reach a truth.

Heptet: A seven-line stanza.

Sestet: A six-line stanza.

1 Explore how the characters in the poem are presented, using quotations and inference, by asking yourself the following questions:

- What do they do?
- What do they value?
- What are the person's feelings towards them?
- How do you know?

(a) On a separate piece of paper, draw a Venn diagram and write the traits inherited from the mother in the circle on the left, those inherited from the father in the circle on the right and those inherited from both in the centre.

CONTINUED ➡

(b) Now create a similar Venn diagram based on the traits you have inherited from your own parents.

2   The R.S. Thomas poem on which 'Inheritance' is based is called 'Gifts'. Find the text online and compare it with Sheers' poem. Make notes on how you think 'Inheritance' has been influenced by 'Gifts', and the ways in which Sheers has developed the original poem.

DEVELOPING YOUR IDEAS

3   Match the quotation to the idea, then use the prompt to explore the quotation.

A slight speech impediment	'joiner's lathe / turning fact into fable' Why the archaic image of a joiner? A fable is a story with a moral message featuring an animal. How else is that applicable here?
A love of the landscape	'testing it under the years' hard hammer' What does this suggest about relationships?
Reverence for physical work and rural pursuits	'a stammer / like a stick in the spokes of my speech' What is the effect of the sibilance here?
An internal conflict	'a need to have my bones near the hill's bare stone' Think about connotations of bones here.

TAKING IT FURTHER

4   The final stanza is shorter than the previous two. Why do you think Sheers has made this choice?

....

....

....

CONTINUED ➤

Answers can be found at: www.hoddereducation.co.uk/workbookanswers

5   Owen Sheers has citied R.S. Thomas' *Selected Poems* as an influence on his work, as these poems introduced him to the 'lonely task' of the poet, 'to return to your failures and make them better'. Sheers also finds inspiration in the poems which find 'significance and metaphor in a rural landscape'.

Record your own response to these ideas, thinking in particular about what Sheers means by the 'metaphor in a rural landscape'.

....

....

....

....

....

....

Challenge yourself

One of R.S. Thomas' most interesting poems is 'A Welsh Testament'. You can easily find the poem online, for example on the Poetry Archive website.
Can you find any examples in Sheers' work that demonstrate a similar ambivalence to Wales and its landscape?

'Marking Time'

STARTING OUT

1   Some students find the violence of this poem somewhat disturbing. Use the space below to find evidence for each point of view.

The poem is a celebration of a couple's irrepressible lust.	The persona displays an unnerving and proprietorial tone towards the woman.

DEVELOPING YOUR IDEAS

2   'Marking time' is a phrase that can suggest both the passage of time and a semantic field of music. Which other words or phrases in the poem link to either of these two possible themes? Why might they have been used?

   (a) Time

   ....

   ....

   ....

   (b) Music

   ....

   ....

   ....

   ....

3   The following quotations describe the woman's skin and the damage caused to it. Match each to the first interpretation, then to another possible suggestion from the second column.

'two tattered flags'	Caused by intense heat	Could also suggest threat beneath.
'brand'	Peaceful and idyllic	Could also suggest decaying and coming to an end.
'still waters'	Proud image	Could also hint at being animalistic.

TAKING IT FURTHER

4   Some of Sheers' poems suggest a much quieter and thoughtful approach to sex. Which poems would make good points of comparisons for this text? Try to name five below:

   ....

   ....

   ....

'Show'

STARTING OUT

1   Summarise each of the two separate sections of this poem as one sentence, thinking about the main theme and narrative in each.

   ●   ....

   ....

   ●   ....

   ....

KEY SKILLS

Being able to concisely summarise a narrative or point of view is invaluable when you are preparing for timed examinations. For each poem you revisit or critical article you read, try to keep very concise notes in the form of two or three sentences on a flashcard. You can use these to revise later.

DEVELOPING YOUR IDEAS

2   **Caesuras** are used throughout the text. In these examples, the pause comes at the line end. Describe how you felt at each pause, and how your feelings changed with the subsequent line.

(a) 'walk, / high-heeled'

At the pause ···

As the next line begins ···

(b) 'walk down the corridor / to wait in the bar for you'

At the pause ···

As the next line begins ···

(c) 'one shoulder bare, / setting the room about you out of focus'

At the pause ···

As the next line begins ···

Caesura: A break or pause in a text, signalled by a line end, comma, semicolon or other method.

3   Read the phrases below. What do the underlined words connote? Think about how they relate to power and admiration.

(a) 'featherless <u>wings</u> / of their <u>shoulders</u>'

···

···

···

(b) '<u>mirror</u> / like a <u>pianist</u>'

···

···

···

TAKING IT FURTHER

4   The two halves of the poem are very different. Underline one of the descriptions below that you agree with the most, and explain your choice.

- The main focus is on the difference between public and private, emphasising the superficiality of modern life and contrasting it with the intensity and realism of private relationships.

- The main focus is on superficial female physical beauty, appreciating women as both vulnerable and strong, as part of a group and then individually.

- The main focus is on how he finds her presence intoxicating and captivating, attractive but also powerful.

....

....

....

....

....

'Valentine'

STARTING OUT

1   The word 'torture' in the first line is unexpected given the suggestion of romance in the title of the poem. What does this suggest about the relationship in the poem.

....

....

....

DEVELOPING YOUR IDEAS

2   The poem is confusing and enigmatic, but probably depicts a romantic break to Paris which has not worked out as planned. For each idea, list the typical connotations and then Sheers' implications.

IDEA	TYPICALLY SUGGESTS	SHEERS SUGGESTS
Paris		

CONTINUED ➤

Answers can be found at: www.hoddereducation.co.uk/workbookanswers

IDEA	TYPICALLY SUGGESTS	SHEERS SUGGESTS
Lover's eyelashes		
High heels		
Couple in bed together		

TAKING IT FURTHER

3   Imagine you are one of the couple. On a separate piece of paper, write a postcard to a close friend describing what has happened on your romantic break.

Challenge yourself

Read the James Fenton poem 'In Paris With You' (try the Poem Hunter website). How is it similar to or different from 'Valentine'? Which do you prefer, and why?

'Winter Swans'*

STARTING OUT

1   (a)   What do swans connote? Gather as many possible ideas in the space below.

(b)   Now highlight in one colour any of your ideas which could also be applicable to icebergs. Repeat with another colour for porcelain.

(c)   What do you notice about the similarities and differences between the three main images of the poem? What could Sheers be saying about relationships?

(d)   On a separate piece of paper, write a paragraph summing up your ideas.

DEVELOPING YOUR IDEAS

For each of Questions 2–7, add a short quotation from the poem, followed by an analysis of the effects created.

2   How is **pathetic fallacy** used by Sheers?

....

....

....

Pathetic fallacy: When a writer uses aspects of nature or weather to suggest the emotion or content of the text. Think about arguments taking place in storms, for example.

3   How does Sheers use sibilance in the second stanza?

....

....

....

4   What is the effect of the description of the birds in the third stanza?

....

....

....

5   What is the effect of the similes in the fourth stanza?

....

....

....

6   What is the effect of the direct speech in the fifth stanza?

....

....

....

7   How is personification used in the sixth stanza?

....

....

....

TAKING IT FURTHER

8 On a separate piece of paper, storyboard the main ideas of the poem. Choose how to divide the poem into eight (not just one box for each of the seven stanzas). Label each box with a short quotation and one abstract noun to show the overriding emotion at that point.

Challenge yourself

Research other important instances of swans in literature. You might like to start with W.B. Yeats' poem 'Wild Swans at Coole'.

Practice examination essay

The previous four poems ('Marking Time', 'Show', 'Valentine' and 'Winter Swans') have offered a range of different ideas about relationships. Using these poems as the basis for your answer, use the structured plan below to formulate an answer to the exam-style question:

'In *Skirrid Hill* relationships are delicate and doomed to fall apart.'

Examine this view of Sheers' presentation of relationships in the collection.

STARTING OUT

Introduction

1 Define terms: *The noun 'relationship' usually means ...* **(AO1: clarity, shaped response)**

....

....

....

In love literature, relationships are usually depicted as ... **(AO4: typicality of ideas and their presentation, and connections across texts)**

....

....

....

In literature of recent decades, relationships have usually been depicted as ... **(AO3: context)**

....

....

....

DEVELOPING YOUR IDEAS

2   Find quotations and give a brief analysis of each quotation to support the idea that relationships are …

●   delicate and fragile

....

....

....

....

●   doomed to fall apart

....

....

....

....

3   Find quotations and give a brief analysis of each quotation to support the idea that relationships are not delicate or falling apart but are in fact …

●   strong

....

....

....

....

●   passionate

....

....

....

....

●   enduring

....

....

....

....

TAKING IT FURTHER

Conclusion

4   Find quotations and give a brief analysis of each quotation to support the following idea **(AO5: different interpretations):**

However, while relationships in 'Skirrid Hill' are often delicate and fragile, there is always a sense of hope and continuity.

....

....

....

....

....

....

....

....

....

If your exam board is WJEC or Eduqas, you are required at AS or A2 to compare Sheers' poetry with Seamus Heaney's *Field Work*. On a separate piece of paper, make brief notes on key quotations from that text which you could incorporate.

'Night Windows'*

STARTING OUT

1   Look at the Moma.org website for images of, and a commentary on, a famous painting by Edward Hopper, also called 'Night Windows'. This painting inspired the setting, though possibly not the action, of the poem.

On a separate piece of paper, describe what you see, or sketch the picture.

2   (a) Circle the statement that best encapsulates your view of the poem.

- The poem is voyeuristic and makes me feel uncomfortable, as the neighbours are clearly watching the couple have sex.
- The poem is romantic and erotic, as the neighbours close the windows to allow the couple privacy.

(b) Which three short quotations from the poem could you use to support your view?

- ....

- ....

- ....

DEVELOPING YOUR IDEAS

3   The poem uses lots of imagery related to light. What do you think each of the following suggests?

   (a) 'the hall bulb bright, / sending one bar of light'

   ....

   ....

   (b) 'their Morse codes, / side-swipes of curtains'

   ....

   ....

   (c) 'a siren's, / sending its blue strobe across the rooftops'

   ....

   ....

4   On a separate piece of paper, draw four boxes. Title the first one 'celebratory', the second one 'awkward' the third 'realistic' and the fourth 'voyeuristic'. Find short quotations from the poem that suggest each mood, and write them in the appropriate box.

TAKING IT FURTHER

5   For each idea below, find two short quotations and explain the effects they create. Write your answers on a separate piece of paper.

   (a) The woman is described as dangerous and her body is described as a weapon.

   (b) The penultimate stanza suggests danger rather than romance.

   (c) He is infatuated with her.

   (d) The act of sex is described as a work of art.

   (e) The woman's feelings at the end of the poem are ambiguous.

'Keyways'*

STARTING OUT

1   Match the definition to the term, thinking about lock mechanisms. (You may find it useful to read a brief history of keys, such as that on Scienceabc.com.)

Edentate	Flat surface of key
Milling	Shape of key
Combinations	Altering a key from blank to specific
Tumblers	Toothless
Bolt	Numerical code for access instead of a key
Blade	Mechanism inside lock

DEVELOPING YOUR IDEAS

2   Thinking again about each of these key-related terms from the poem, what other connotations do they have? What does each suggest about the relationship being depicted in the poem?

Edentate	
Milling	
Combinations	
Tumblers	
Bolt	
Blade	

3   Each of the separate episodes in the poem further develops our understanding of the phases of their relationship which has brought them to this point, where they are exchanging keys so that he can remove his belongings.

For each episode, write a sentence paraphrasing how he felt about that moment. Write your answers on a separate piece of paper.

(a) Standing in the locksmiths at the end of the relationship

(b) Listening to Handel's *Messiah* (a piece of classical music) in a chapel

(c) In bed together

4   For each episode, analyse the effect of the key word quoted from that part. Write your answers on a separate piece of paper.

(a) Standing in the locksmiths at the end of the relationship: 'presses'

(b) Listening to Handel's *Messiah* (a piece of classical music) in a chapel: 'unison'

(c) In bed together: 'home'

TAKING IT FURTHER

5 Critic Sarah Crown referred to *Skirrid Hill* as 'a gorgeously elegiac volume'. How far would you agree that this poem is an **elegy** to a failed relationship? You can read the rest of the article on the *Guardian* website by entering 'Sarah Crown Sheers' in the search box.

....

....

....

Elegy: In classical literature, a poem written in couplets, often with a mournful or wistful tone. In modern poetry, a poem that laments the dead or reflects in a serious tone.

6 Do you think 'Keyways' is characteristic of the collection as a whole? Which other poems in the collection do you feel are elegiac?

....

....

....

'Border Country'*

STARTING OUT

1 The poem is about a friend of the persona, whose farming father killed himself. Similar cases were reported by the BBC and other news organisations in Wales in the 1990s and early 2000s, with problems in agriculture exacerbated by animal ailments such as foot and mouth disease.
On a separate piece of paper, make brief notes on these issues; you can try searching the internet using prompts like 'BBC farmer death foot and mouth' but be aware that, like the poem, some stories will be upsetting.

2 Circle the idea that fits more closely with your own perception of the poem, and explain your choice in the space below.

● The poem is more about the persona growing up and losing touch with his teenage rural self.

● The poem is more about the tragic story of the friend and his father's death.

....

....

....

....

DEVELOPING YOUR IDEAS

3   The poem uses lots of nature imagery. For each of the quotations below, consider the possible connotations.

(a) 'elephant'

....

....

(b) 'minnows'

....

....

(c) 'pumpkins'

....

....

(d) 'buzzards'

....

....

(e) 'poppy'

....

....

(f) 'sheep'

....

....

(g) 'cows'

....

....

4   **Prolepsis** is used, in the form of a number of images, nouns, verbs and adjectives in the first four stanzas, to foreshadow the father's death at the end of the fourth stanza. List the five most important examples below.

....

....

Prolepsis: A flashforward or foreshadowing effect in literature. The opposite is **analepsis**.

TAKING IT FURTHER

5   Some stanzas are more uplifting and positive than others, where the focus is more on death and decline. On a separate piece of paper, draw a tension graph of the poem, annotating each change of direction with a single-word quotation. (If you haven't drawn a tension graph before, search online for 'tension graph template' to see examples.)

Challenge yourself

This poem is about a literal border country – that is, on the edge of both England and Wales – but also about metaphorical borders, such as childhood and adolescence. What other borders can you think of that can be inferred from the text?

'Farther'

STARTING OUT

1   The title of the poem is a pun and uses a homophone. 'Farther' means increasingly far away, but sounds like 'father'. How far apart are the father and son in each of these examples? On a separate piece of paper, draw a horizontal line with 'closest' written at one end and 'furthest apart' at the other. Write each quotation at the appropriate point on the line and add notes to explore imagery and lexis for each.

'We stopped there'   'find you in its frame'

'together'   'with every step apart, I'm another closer to you'

'you are with me again'   'I turned to look at you'

'a father's grief / at the loss of his son to man'

> Homophone: Pair of words that sound alike but are spelled differently and have different meanings.
> Homonym: Pair of words that sound alike but have different meanings.
> Homograph: Pair of words that are spelled the same but may sound different and have different meanings.

2   Rank the adjectives below (from 1 for the word that best suits your feelings about the poem, to 5 for the word that is least like your ideas).

Mournful ____   Cheerful ____   Triumphant ____   Poignant ____   Calm ____

DEVELOPING YOUR IDEAS

3   Much of the poem is written without thorough punctuation. Using a pencil, annotate a copy of the poem to show where one could insert commas, full stops, dashes or semicolons.

 CONTINUED ➡

4 What is the effect of Sheers omitting them?

....

....

....

5 Now choose five short quotations that best prove your choice of the most important adjective from Question 2, and describe the effect of each.

QUOTATION	EFFECT

TAKING IT FURTHER

6   Although the story of the poem is simple (a man and his father walk up the Skirrid hill amicably), some of the imagery is more subtle and ambiguous. Match the quotation to the subject and then make notes on the effect.

DESCRIPTION/METAPHOR	SUBJECT	EFFECT
'its puzzle solved by moss'	Cave or rocks	
'altar'	The intersection of sky and mountains on the horizon	
'the sound of a crowd sighing'	Seeing the landscape	
'shock [...] unrolled'	Hopeful feeling when thinking about his relationship with his father	
'rubbed raw'	The dry stone wall	
'shallow handhold'	Sound of the stones shifting underfoot	

7   What qualities of his father are described in this poem? Answer true, false or possibly (in your opinion) to each. Then add a quotation from the poem to justify your idea, and finally add two synonyms for the adjective, working on broadening your critical vocabulary.

(a) Old ....

....

(b) Sympathetic ....

....

(c) Nature loving ....

....

(d) Youthful ....

....

CONTINUED ➡

(e) Mysterious ....

....

8   Think back to the poem 'Inheritance'. How is this poem similar or different in terms of the way the father is described? On which quotations from the poems are you basing this? Write your answer on a separate piece of paper.

'Trees'

STARTING OUT

1   (a) What do oak trees symbolise, and for what have they been historically used?

....

....

(b) How does that relate to this poem?

....

....

DEVELOPING YOUR IDEAS

2   Add three brief quotations for each viewpoint.

	The poem celebrates the planting of a new tree and the subsequent promise and hope of watching it grow in a landscape the persona holds dear.	The persona realises with a shock the future death of his father, and the brief and ephemeral qualities of human life: the tree will outlast them both.
A		
B		
C		

3   Which of the statements above do you think best describes the intention of the poem? Rewrite the statement in your own words below.

....

....

....

CONTINUED ➡

4   Now, on a separate piece of paper, write a paragraph that includes your quotations and analysis from the opposing view in Question 2. Begin your paragraph like this:

However, a different reading could be that ...

TAKING IT FURTHER

5   Listen to Philip Larkin read his poem 'The Trees' on the Poetry Archive website.

The second line is key. On a separate piece of paper, explain what you think the father in the poem is trying to say by planting the new tree.

'Hedge School'*

STARTING OUT

1   Research hedge schools online and complete the paragraph below.

A hedge school is a name given to an .... practice in the .... and .... centuries in places like .... Lessons were usually held in .... because laws had been passed which made it illegal to .... because .... Hedge schools are often seen to represent .... and .... In post-1945 literature, the concept has been explored most thoroughly in .... by ...., a .... in which the playwright examines ideas about Irish .... and ....

2   The implication of the poem is that one can learn a great deal from nature and from unexpected scenarios, people and places. What does Sheers learn on his walk?

....

....

....

DEVELOPING YOUR IDEAS

3   The persona outlines three possible choices when faced with a handful of blackberries. For each, select and analyse the most important short quotation.

Eating them straight away, one by one

CONTINUED ➡

Eating them in one handful

Squashing them in a fist

TAKING IT FURTHER

The poem is prefaced by a quotation from Geoffrey Chaucer's thirteenth-century *Canterbury Tales*.

Modern translation

I rekke nevere, whan that thet been beryed,

I never care, when they've been buried,

Though that hir soules goon a-blakeberyed!

If their souls go blackberrying [go to hell].

Chaucer's message is that people are easily corruptible and that human nature is inherently flawed; people are easily led astray.

4 How far does Chaucer's message coincide with Sheers' ideas about the young boy in his poem?

....

....

....

....

....

5 Sheers has cited Seamus Heaney an influence on his work. Read Heaney's poem 'Blackberry Picking' in full on the Poetry Foundation website. Select the five most striking words or phrases in the poem and then compare them with five from Sheers' poem that either echo or refute Heaney's ideas.

HEANEY	SHEERS

CONTINUED ➡

<table>
<tr><td></td><td></td></tr>
<tr><td></td><td></td></tr>
<tr><td></td><td></td></tr>
</table>

Challenge yourself

Sylvia Plath (a 1950s American confessional poet) also wrote about blackberries. Find her poem 'Blackberrying' online. What is the main message here? How does it compare with Sheers' poem?

Practice examination essay

The previous four poems ('Border Country', 'Farther', 'Trees' and 'Hedge School') have offered a range of different ideas about nature. Using these poems as the basis for your answer, use the structured plan below to formulate an answer to the exam-style question:

'In *Skirrid Hill*, nature replaces God.'

Examine this view of Sheers' presentation of nature in the collection.

STARTING OUT

Introduction

1 (a) Define terms: The noun 'nature' usually means … **(AO1: clarity, shaped response)**

....

....

(b) One major literary movement concerning the intersection of nature and religion was the Romantics, active from the late eighteenth to mid-nineteenth century and including famous writers like William Wordsworth, John Keats and Mary Shelley. Their main view on the two themes was that ....

....

.... **(AO4: typicality)**

(c) In most twentieth-century literature, nature is depicted as … **(AO4: typicality)**

....

....

DEVELOPING YOUR IDEAS

2   Find quotations and give a brief analysis of each quotation to support the idea that nature replaces God. **(AO2: analysis of language, structure and form)**

   (a)   Nature displays godlike qualities such as omnipotence, omniscience and omnibenevolence. **(AO1: terminology and expression)**

....

....

....

....

   (b)   Nature is parental in the collection: protecting, nourishing and encouraging.

....

....

....

....

   (c)   Nature is dependable and cyclical. **(AO2: analysis of structure and form of poems and the whole collection in particular, such as the placement of 'Border Country' within the collection)**

....

....

....

....

3   Find quotations and give a brief analysis of each quotation to support the idea that nature doesn't replace God.

   (a) In Sheers' work, humans are more powerful than nature.

....

....

....

....

CONTINUED ➔

(b) Human *decisions and actions, such as war, overpower nature.* **(Include some AO3 social and historical context here, such as the First World War)**

....

....

....

....

....

TAKING IT FURTHER

Conclusion

4   Find quotations and give a brief analysis of each quotation to support the following idea. **(AO5: debate)**

However, the focus of the collection is on the transformative and profound quality of human relationships, and nature and landscape are simply metaphors for this idea.

....

....

....

....

....

If you are taking the WJEC or Eduqas exam, you are required at AS or A2 to compare Sheers with another text, such as Heaney, so on a separate piece of paper make brief notes on key quotations from that text that you could incorporate.

'Joseph Jones'*

STARTING OUT

1   Consider the connotations of these popular cultural references:

(a) (Hair) 'gel'...

....

(b) 'red wings'...

....

CONTINUED ➡

(c) 'skirt [...] blown inside out'..

....

(d) 'XR2'...

....

2   Cumulatively, what kind of character is Joseph Jones? List ten adjectives to describe him.

....

....

....

....

DEVELOPING YOUR IDEAS

3   This poem is narrated in a conversational tone, as if answering a question unheard by the reader. For each aspect of this tone, describe the effect created, filling in the boxes of these PEA paragraphs.

POINT	EXAMPLE	ANALYSIS
Sheers opens the poem with an emphatic statement in the first line.		
		Omitting certain words in a sentence gives the effect that …
The persona lists nouns without linking words – a technique called asyndeton.		
	'he', 'Her'	

TAKING IT FURTHER

4   Line breaks and spacing are used to create important effects in this poem. Using the prompts below, label your text with suggestions of which effect is created in each space. Use the underlined words as a short way of annotating.

-   Show time for persona to <u>reflect or reminisce</u>.

-   Recreate Joseph Jones' <u>unhurried</u> attitude.

-   Allow for a <u>poignant</u> reflection.

-   Increase a sense of <u>litotes</u> or understatement: his achievements are underwhelming.

-   Hint at a <u>seedy or sexual</u> image without explaining.

5   The poem has an ambiguous tone: at first it seems to celebrate Jones, but on closer inspection there is an irony, too. For each quotation, explain how it could be used to argue each point of view.

JONES IS CELEBRATED	QUOTATION	JONES IS MOCKED
	'hair sheened with gel'	
	'air dead with scent'	
	'small town myth'	

Challenge yourself

Are material possessions integral to identity? What are the most important objects and moments in defining your own identity? What do they say about you?

'Late Spring'

STARTING OUT

1 Circle the statement that best sums up your reaction to the poem. Then, using the space below, explain why you have chosen your statement using quotations.

- The poem is horrifying: the animals are deprived of any sexual function and yet are described in a variety of euphemistic ways, with the child narrator unaware of the implications of their actions.

- The poem is poignant: the everyday reality of framing is being seen afresh through poetic and unexpected metaphors, and a close focus on a touching moment between boy and grandfather.

....

....

....

DEVELOPING YOUR IDEAS

2 The poem uses **phallic imagery** for a variety of reasons. Match the quotations to the potential effects created. You may find that one quotation has more than one effect, and vice versa.

QUOTATION
'the made-to-purpose-tool, / heavy and steel-hard'
'two soaped beans into a delicate purse'
'clenched fist'
'crown them'

EFFECT CREATED
Implies potential for violence and impulsive behaviour
Suggests a patriarchal society
Reinforces stereotype of masculine work
Makes a more subtle point about gender and expectations

Phallic imagery: An image that implies masculine sexual power and is shaped like a penis. (noun: phallus)
Yonic: Imagery representative of female power and resembling a vulva.

TAKING IT FURTHER

3 On a separate piece of paper, make notes on how this poem compares with 'The Farrier' in its presentation of **(a)** masculinity and **(b)** nature.

Challenge yourself

How does Sheers define masculinity in this poem? How does this compare with another poet explored in your wider reading or comparative text such as Seamus Heaney or R.S. Thomas? Make a list of key quotations and ideas on this topic from each writer.

'The Equation'*

STARTING OUT

1 On a separate piece of paper, draw four boxes. Title the first one 'magic', the second one 'maths and education' the third 'nature and farming' and the fourth 'senses'. Fill in the boxes with quotations from the poem on each theme.

DEVELOPING YOUR IDEAS

2 In some ways, this poem can be seen as the companion piece to 'Late Spring', which comes immediately prior to it in the collection. For each idea, choose a quotation from each poem to explore.

'LATE SPRING'	POINT OF COMPARISON	'THE EQUATION'
	Admiring the grandfather	
	Strange comparisons and oxymoron	
	Reality versus illusions	
	The effect on the animals	

KEY SKILLS

You need to be aware of how the collection as a whole functions and is structured, not just each poem.

3 On a separate piece of paper, rewrite the poem from the point of view of the grandfather, trying to infer his thoughts and feelings from the observations of the persona. Use quotations from the original if you can.

TAKING IT FURTHER

4   In an interview in 2005 with Lisa Gee of *The Independent*, Sheers said that although his poems may 'take their initial spark' from his own life, they do not merely recount an event. He said,

> A poem is not worth putting out into the world unless that personal experience is going to resonate with other people. It has to be a crafted piece of work. And, in the end, while it will still have links to me and my life, there's almost as much imagination and invention in any first-person poem as there is in a first-person novel.

On a separate piece of paper, explain how this changes your reading of this poem or the rest of the collection.

Challenge yourself

Read the whole article on the *Independent* website (search for 'Blue-eyed boy and bard Sheers') and write down five more phrases or ideas that are useful in furthering your understanding of Sheers' work.

'Swallows'

STARTING OUT

1   Why do you think Sheers has chosen to focus on swallows?

....

....

2   Circle the words which best fit your understanding of the qualities Sheers is trying to convey through his metaphor.

authoritative	collective	creative	darting
ephemeral	eternal	individual	insignificant
rapid	significant	swooping	

DEVELOPING YOUR IDEAS

3   The **eponymous** swallows represent the cyclical and regenerative cycle of life. Look at the middle stanza and explain what is suggested by each of these quotations.

(a) 'annual regeneration'

....

....

....

CONTINUED ➔

(b) 'no seam / between parent and child'

....

....

....

....

(c) 'flawless to human eyes'

....

....

....

Eponymous: Relating to the thing or person named in the title. (**Anonymous** means not identified by name.)

TAKING IT FURTHER

4   Other key bird references in the collection include the curlews of 'Show' and the 'Winter Swans'. Use these poems to write analytical paragraphs based on the statements below. Write your paragraphs on a separate piece of paper.

(a) Sheers uses bird imagery to emphasise femininity in the collection.

(b) Sheers uses bird imagery to reinforce the power of nature in the collection.

(c) Sheers uses bird imagery as a way of exploring the idea of human love and romance.

'On Going'*

STARTING OUT

1   Before the poem starts, Sheers has included a dedication: 'i.m. Jean Sheers'. With this in mind, the title 'On Going' can be read in two ways. Circle the one you find more convincing and explain your choice in the space below.

● 'On going' means this is a continuing or endless process; he continues to suffer and think about her death.

● 'On going' means this poem is about the finality of her 'going' – a euphemism for dying.

....

....

i.m. *in memoriam*, Latin for 'in memory'.

CONTINUED ➡

2   The poem is written in four stanzas, each with a subtle shift in focus.

On a separate piece of paper, outline briefly the main ideas in each stanza, and use the suggested words below to describe the tone of each part. What happens, what is the tense and what is the focus?

delicate	detached	disconcerting	distant
emotional	fragile	involved	pensive

poignant	scientific	thoughtful

DEVELOPING YOUR IDEAS

3   Sheers uses unexpected images and description in this poem. For each quotation, explain the possible effects created.

(a) 'windows into the soul's temperature'

....

....

....

(b) 'an ancient child'

....

....

....

(c) 'breath working at the skin of your cheek'

....

....

....

(d) 'your paper temple'

....

....

....

(e) 'the sleep of their slow-closing'

....

....

....

TAKING IT FURTHER

4 Find and read Dylan Thomas' poem 'Do Not Go Gentle into that Good Night'. Whereas Sheers' account of his grandmother's death is almost eerily peaceful, Thomas' poem is a complete contrast, angrily inciting the addressee to resist death. Compare the two poems, using the prompts below.

PROMPT	THOMAS' POEM	SHEERS' POEM
Opening line and tone		
Key verbs		
Key imagery		
Use of structure		
Closing line and tone		

KEY SKILLS

Remember that your examination is likely to include an element of unseen texts, for which you will need to understand the main ideas, tone and techniques in a poem quickly.

'Y Gaer'* and 'The Hill Fort'*

STARTING OUT

Sheers deliberately placed 'The Hill Fort' and its companion piece 'Y Gaer' facing each other at the very heart of his *Skirrid Hill* collection. This suggests looking forward and back, viewing things in two ways simultaneously, and being two people at once (the names are the same but one is in English and one in Welsh).

1   Which of the two following descriptions better explains your feelings on these two poems? Sheers has said that he wrote the two poems after a family friend lost teenage son in a car accident.

   ● The poems are needlessly sentimental and self-consciously poetic.

   ● The poems are an effective exploration of a man's grief and the use of two perspectives is thought-provoking and subtle.

2   What is the significance of having the two titles in English and Welsh? Circle the explanation with which you agree more:

   ● These represent the dual identity that Sheers and the protagonists feel, as both British and Welsh.

   ● The names are used to show how one place can have different meanings; the archaic name 'Y Gaer' may also suggest how a place can evolve over time in an altered form, as the father's feelings do.

DEVELOPING YOUR IDEAS

Sheers sees landscape as a way to explore relationships between people, and between people and their world. The critic Sarah Crown, says:

> The ruptured terrain reflects the collection's fractured emotional landscape. Things are falling apart in these poems: Sheers's subjects range from ageing and loss to the jarring transition between youth and adulthood and the disintegration of relationships […] the pervading atmosphere of breakdown throws into poignant relief the occasional poems in which gaps are bridged or people joined.

Write your answers to these questions on a separate piece of paper.

3   What do you think Crown means by an 'emotional landscape'?

4   Which quotations in these two poems and the rest of the collection are brought to mind by this phrase?

5   Is the 'pervading atmosphere' in this collection one of breakdown? Make a list of poems below to support this view, and a list of poems which would refute this view.

CONTINUED ➡

6   What 'gaps are bridged' in these two poems?

7   What is the significance of the hill fort? Make notes on why you think Sheers chose this particular setting to explore ideas about a man and his bereavement.

8   Explore each of these quotations from 'Y Gaer', considering what sounds and images are used, and what Sheers wants the reader to feel and think about at that point in the text:

   (a) 'stone pile marking' ....

   ....

   ....

   (b) 'an answer to any question' ....

   ....

   ....

   (c) 'lean full tilt / against the wind's shoulder' ....

   ....

   ....

   (d) 'something huge enough to blame' ....

   ....

   ....

9   Explore each of these quotations from 'The Hill Fort':

   (a) 'wild as the long-maned ponies' ....

   ....

   ....

   (b) 'by the fathers and sons before them' ....

   ....

   ....

   (c) 'we're no more than scattered grains' ....

   ....

   ....

   (d) 'the depth of their impression' ....

   ....

   ....

CONTINUED ➔

Answers can be found at: www.hoddereducation.co.uk/workbookanswers

(e) 'these ashes' ....

....

....

(f) 'tongue of the wind' ....

....

....

TAKING IT FURTHER

Critic Olivia Coles prefers the bleakly arresting end of the first poem, with the father trying to cope with bereavement, to what she sees as the overly neat ending of its companion poem.

10 Which poem do you prefer, and why? On a separate piece of paper, write a paragraph to explain your choice. Try to consider imagery and structure, including sound and rhyme, in your response.

Challenge yourself

Listen to the two poems read aloud at the Owen Sheers page of the Poetry Archive website. What do you notice about the sounds and rhymes that is not immediately evident on the page?

'Intermission'*

STARTING OUT

1 The idea of an interval or intermission suggests a performance. Name five poems in the collection that also deal with ideas of performing.

....

....

2 Before you tackle the more detailed questions, record your first thoughts on the poem below, thinking about what is most memorable to you.

Feelings	Images
Words	Sounds

Challenge yourself

Think about the etymology of the noun 'intermission'. It comes from two Latin words: the prefix *inter* meaning 'between' and the verb *mittere* meaning 'to let go'. What ideas and themes have characterised the first half of the collection? What might Sheers be letting go of before the second half commences?

DEVELOPING YOUR IDEAS

3   The poem describes a house where two friends are talking during a power cut. What adjectives could you use to characterise the atmosphere?

....

....

4   How does that change during the poem?

....

....

5   Comment on each of the following quotations, explaining how it contributes to this effect.

(a) 'wells of darkness' ....

....

....

(b) 'mine shafts of night' ....

....

....

(c) 'firelight' ....

....

....

(d) 'shrunken' ....

....

....

6   (a) Which line in the poem uses **bathos**?

....

CONTINUED ➡

(b) How do you feel about its inclusion? Does it detract from the overall effectiveness of the poem?

....

....

....

....

Bathos: A deliberate shift from the serious to the silly.

TAKING IT FURTHER

7   Critics such as Sarah Crown in the *Guardian* have said that one weakness of Sheers' poetry is a tendency to insist on the message of poems, and a reluctance to trust the reader to work out his meaning. Do you agree?

  (a) On a separate piece of paper, write one paragraph where you agree, citing particular poems and lines to argue your case.

  (b) Now write a second paragraph where you disagree with Crown's critique, citing particular poems and lines to argue your case.

Challenge yourself

Read the review on the *Guardian* website (search for 'Sarah Crown Owen Sheers review') and note down five key phrases or sentences that further your understanding of the collection.

'Calendar'

STARTING OUT

1   Look up the definitions of the Haiku techniques 'Kiru' and 'Kigo'. Does Sheers use these techniques? Or does Sheers stray from the typical haiku form? Use evidence to support your answer.

....

....

....

....

DEVELOPING YOUR IDEAS

2   Which word in each stanza do you think is the most effective at creating the given effect, and why?

(a) Spring: a feeling of excitement and promise

....

....

(b) Summer: a feeling of romance

....

....

(c) Autumn: a feeling of quiet contemplation

....

....

(d) Winter: a feeling of death and decay

....

....

3   Each stanza contains one particularly arresting image. For each, write notes on the connotations of each constituent word and the overall effect created.

(a) 'sing volts' ....

....

....

(b) 'down at the / lips of foxgloves' ....

....

....

(c) 'danced / a fingerprint' ....

....

....

(d) 'the rooks are a / passing infection' ....

....

....

CONTINUED ➡

TAKING IT FURTHER

4   What do you think is the message of the poem?

....

....

....

5   Which poem more closely resembles 'Calendar' in terms of outlook and message: 'Trees' or 'Swallows'? On a separate piece of paper, write a paragraph to explain your answer, using quotations from all three poems.

'Flag'*

STARTING OUT

1   Write the definition next to each word.

WORD	DEFINITION
Tercets	
Epigraph	
Bipartite	
Nationalism	
Identity	

2   When and where do you most often see your own national flag? What are your own feelings towards it? On a separate piece of paper, draw a brief concept map or wordle as a way of collating your own ideas about flags. Do you think this would be the same for people from different generations and classes?

DEVELOPING YOUR IDEAS

3   The poem begins with an extract from Christopher Logue's poem 'Professor Tucholsky's Facts'. Find out more about this poem and record your ideas about why Sheers may have chosen to use it to preface his poem.

....

....

....

....

....

4   Sheers' poem explores a range of feelings toward the flag and the country it represents. For each word quoted below, identify the part of speech (e.g. adverb) and tense (for verbs), and suggest the effect created.

(a) 'start' ....

....

(b) 'our' ....

....

(c) 'fading' ....

....

(d) 'fits' ....

....

(e) 'beast' ....

....

(f) 'fiction' ....

....

(g) 'pulsing' ....

....

(h) 'staunching' ....

....

CONTINUED ➡

5   On a separate piece of paper, draw a horizontal line with 'negative' written at one end and 'positive' at the other. Write each of the words from Question 4 at the appropriate point on the line, according to how positive or negative the feeling is that they express. Add five more words from the poem that also convey Sheers' feelings.

TAKING IT FURTHER

6   For each of the following viewpoints, record the five most relevant quotations and briefly analyse them. Write your answers on a separate piece of paper.

   (a) The poem is about how the flag has come to represent misguided aims and ideals: it is only seen in run-down areas and is less relevant in the modern world.

   (b) The poem is nostalgic about the flag: although it is only seen in dilapidated places, it still represents optimism and hope for a more economically prosperous and proud future for Wales.

7   Of the two views in Question 6, circle the one you find more convincing. On a separate piece of paper, write a paragraph to explain your views, using at least five brief quotations from the poem to do so.

8   Search for the British-Guyanese poet John Agard's poem, also called 'Flag'. (The BBC GCSE Bitesize website has a video of him reading it which may help you understand his accent and delivery.) Make brief notes on the two poems in the space below.

	SHEERS	AGARD
Main viewpoint and tone		
Key quotations and analysis		

'The Steelworks'*

STARTING OUT

Read the article and look at the accompanying pictures from the BBC online article 'The Last Shift at Ebbw Vale', from February 2017.

1   What do you notice about the sex, ethnicity and names of the workers?

   ....

   ....

CONTINUED ➡

2   The poem is unusual in that the title forms part of the first line. How would you define the tone
    established in this first sentence, and is it characteristic of Sheers' work?

    ....

    ....

    ....

DEVELOPING YOUR IDEAS

3   Match the idea to the quotation.

'The Steelworks, / except it doesn't anymore'	The use of science fiction imagery lends a surreal and disbelieving tone.
'deserted mothership'	Pathetic fallacy and industrial imagery reiterate a tone of despondency and nostalgia.
'the rain, / rolling off the clouds in sheets'	Religious imagery shows the men's need to establish a purpose for themselves in the absence of the camaraderie and industry of the steelworks.
'benediction of a lateral pull'	Unusually for Sheers, the title is part of the poem, separated from the rest of the sentence with a comma. He uses a pun to establish a tone of discontent and dark humour.

4   Colour code a copy of the poem, looking for:

●   religious imagery

●   science fiction imagery

●   pathetic fallacy.

5   Which of these three is most important?

    ....

6   What effect does it create?

    ....

    ....

    ....

    ....

TAKING IT FURTHER

7   For this 'Point' sentence, add evidence and analysis.

Sheers begins the poem with a description of the works to show how outsiders may not understand the remains of the buildings, and what they represent.

....

....

....

....

8   Use the bullet points below to complete the sentences (or use your own ideas). Then develop the ideas further.
   ● emphasises the passage of time and the lack of activity in a once bustling environment.
   ● reveals the poet's respect for the men and his sadness at the closing of the steelworks.
   ● is typical of his view of masculinity.

   (a) The use of verbs in the second stanza ...

   ....

   ....

   ....

   ....

   (b) The ambiguity of the noun 'work' and the description in the penultimate stanza ...

   ....

   ....

   ....

   ....

   (c) Sheers' refusal to describe the emotions of the men and decision to focus on their actions ...

   ....

   ....

   ....

   ....

Challenge yourself

In the absence of church or work, what do men do with their time? How is this different for women? Why? Has this always been true? Is it different in different parts of the country or world? Consider how society has changed in the past one hundred years as you make your notes. Read the *Guardian* article on Ebbw Vale, '"There's no life here": a journey into Britain's precarious future' (16 December 2017), to find out more about changing society and community in industrial towns.

'Song'

STARTING OUT

1   Sheers uses lots of very negative imagery in an otherwise romantic and positive poem. For each of the quotations below, jot down your own ideas about what qualities or ideas he is suggesting that give the poem a greater complexity and depth than may be apparent at first.

(a) 'bait' ....

....

....

(b) 'siren' ....

....

....

(c) 'oil spill' ....

....

....

(d) 'wring' ....

....

....

(e) 'mites' ....

....

....

DEVELOPING YOUR IDEAS

2   The poem is more like a song with its tercets, than a conventional ballad. Annotate a copy of the poem to suggest which lines you would emphasise with volume or different instruments if you were setting it to music. On a separate piece of paper, make notes to sum up the feelings you would want to get across in your musical version.

TAKING IT FURTHER

3   One of the most striking lines of the poem is 'Love is all there is to save'. Make a list below of the poems in the collection that agree or disagree with the statement, in your view.

AGREE	DISAGREE

4   On a separate piece of paper, write one or more paragraphs comparing how Sheers presents love in this and one other poem in the collection.

'Landmark'*

STARTING OUT

1   Before you analyse the poem in greater depth, gather your initial thoughts by placing quotations and your ideas in the boxes below. This will help you develop a sense of debate about a text which – at first – seems straightforward.

In the poem, love is eternal.	In the poem, love is fleeting.
The poem is optimistic and celebratory.	The poem is ironic and pessimistic.

DEVELOPING YOUR IDEAS

2   For each of the key words below, specify which part of speech it is, and its effect in this poem. Wherever possible, identify two possible interpretations.

(a) 'timeless'

....

....

....

....

(b) 'blackthorn'

....

....

....

....

(c) 'clumsy'

....

....

....

....

(d) 'been'

....

....

....

....

(e) 'complete'

....

....

....

....

3   What is the effect of the third person plural in Sheers' poem?

....

....

TAKING IT FURTHER

4   How useful is the term 'postlapsarian' to your understanding of 'Landmark'?

....

....

Postlapsarian: After the fall of Adam and Eve from grace in the Garden of Eden, when they became aware of nudity and shame after disobeying God.

5   Carol Ann Duffy has said of her own work that, 'Poetry, above all, is a series of intense moments – its power is not in narrative. I'm not dealing with facts, I'm dealing with emotion.' Explain how far you agree that the poem 'Landmark' deals more with facts than emotion.

....

....

....

Challenge yourself

Duffy's 2007 collection *Rapture* provides an excellent counterpoint to Sheers. Read more about her on the Poetry Archive website and about *Rapture* in particular. There is a good review on the *Guardian* website by Margaret Reynolds from 2006. The poem 'Rapture' is similar in terms of context to Sheers' 'Landmark', but with a very different perspective. Read the poem and make notes on how their style and viewpoint differ.

'Happy Accidents'

STARTING OUT

1   Find out more about Robert Capa and the famous photos being described here. You might like to use Mia Tramz's article, 'Robert Capa's Iconic D-Day Photo of a Soldier in the Surf', on the *Time* magazine website. On a separate piece of paper, record key dates, facts and ideas.

2   The title and first line of the poem are ambiguous in several ways. Annotate them closely below, thinking about as many different interpretations as you can of who is talking and what exactly they mean.

Happy Accidents

And Robert Capa, how was he to know?

DEVELOPING YOUR IDEAS

3 Read the poem again and highlight what seem to you to be the twenty key words.

4 Now, on a separate piece of paper, rewrite the poem as a short piece of prose in the voice of Robert Capa himself, explaining the process and his feelings towards the day and the final images.

5 Write the definition next to each of these terms.

Pathos	
Rhetorical question	
Colloquialism	
Half-rhyme	
Sibilance	

6 For each of the following short quotations, explain the effect created. Use the terminology from Question 5 in your answers if you can.

(a) 'And Robert Capa, how was he to know?'

....

....

(b) 'some lad, barely sixteen'

....

(c) 'describe so perfectly'

....

....

(d) 'the trapdoor of war'

....

....

TAKING IT FURTHER

7   Find Carol Ann Duffy's poem 'War Photographer'.

Focus on the six lines that begin 'He has a job to do'. What do you think her view is of the role of a war photographer?

....

....

....

....

8   How is this poem different in tone from Sheers'?

....

....

....

....

9   Revisit Sheers' poem 'Mametz Wood'. Comparing this with 'Happy Accidents', which poem do you find more effective as an evocation of the atmosphere of war? Why? On a separate piece of paper, write a comparative paragraph, using at least four short quotations from each poem.

'Drinking with Hitler'

STARTING OUT

This poem has a specific date and place, suggesting that it was inspired by a real encounter. 'Hitler' is the late Dr 'Hitler' Hunzvi, who was the leader of the Zimbabwe National Liberation War Veterans Association, who put pressure on President Robert Mugabe to improve conditions for those who had served in the Zimbabwe army. This included holding the country's commercial farmers to ransom.

It was later revealed that Hunzvi misused public funds by claiming to be more disabled than he was. Notably, Hunzvi's wife claimed he had mistreated her, so she fled Zimbabwe in 1992. In the course of his travels, Sheers met one of Hunzvi's bodyguards who privately admitted to being an admirer of Cripps' life and achievements.

1   Why do you think the poem ends with the encounter with the woman?

....

....

....

2   What message do you think Sheers is trying to convey by including this poem in the collection?

....

....

....

DEVELOPING YOUR IDEAS

3   Look at the structure of the poem. What shift in tone and topic is created at these points in the poem?

(a)   'He wears' ....

....

....

(b)   'Turning to me' ....

....

....

(c)   'So finished with me' ....

....

....

(d)   'Conducting' ....

....

....

(e)   'She returns' ....

....

....

TAKING IT FURTHER

4   Who is powerful in this poem? Why? Find quotations to support your ideas and then decide on a rank order (from 1 for the most powerful to 3 for the least powerful).

CHARACTER	QUOTATIONS AND IDEAS	RANK
Dr 'Hitler' Hunzvi		
Persona (Sheers)		

CONTINUED ➡

Woman at the bar		

Challenge yourself

Which other poems in the collection could be described as postcolonial? How might your research into **postcolonialism** change your reading of 'Flag', for example?

Postcolonialism: The study of the cultural legacy of colonialism and imperialism, especially looking at the human consequences of the control and exploitation of colonised people and places.

KEY SKILLS

Being aware of the main schools of literary critical thought can be a good starting point for exploring different interpretations. Make sure you understand the rudiments of the following theories and look out for poems that might be particularly relevant to them:

- Feminist
- Marxist
- Postcolonial
- Psychoanalytical

'Four Movements in the Scale of Two'

STARTING OUT

1 The poem uses a **conceit** of music at first. Match the musical terms to the definitions.

CLEF	A set of notes in order, ascending or descending.
MOVEMENT	From the French for key, a symbol showing the pitch of notes on a stave.
SCALE	A separate section of a longer musical work. Traditionally the four sections were fast, slow, dance-like and then fast to finish.

Conceit: A metaphor or comparison running throughout a text, as Sheers does here with the idea of him being a magpie. You might like to compare this with John Donne's famous poem 'The Flea'.

2 The poem is in four sections. Look at the titles of each: what do they suggest to you?

(a) 'Pages' ....

....

....

(b) 'Still Life'...

....

CONTINUED ➡

(c) 'Eastern Promise' ....
....
....

(d) 'Line-Break'...
....
....

DEVELOPING YOUR IDEAS

3 For each of these key quotations, explain the possible effect created.

(a) 'Cut to us' ....
....
....

(b) 'back to naked back' ....
....
....

(c) 'bodies, like souls' ....
....
....

(d) 'until the words caught her' ....
....
....

(e) 'dull-snapping'...
....
....

(f) 'slow smoke-signal'...
....
....

TAKING IT FURTHER

4 This is one of the most abstract and unusually structured poems in the collection. Do you think it is effective? On a separate piece of paper write a paragraph defending your view.

'Liable to Floods'

1   The phrase 'liable to floods' is an example of **litotes**.

(a) What does 'liable to floods' usually suggest?

....

(b) What is the broader message of the poem that Sheers is trying to convey?

....

....

(c) On a separate piece of paper, write a paragraph in which you answer the mini-question
**'What does the poem "Liable to Floods" uniquely add to the collection?' Use evidence from this
poem and elsewhere in the text to justify your ideas.**

Litotes: Understatement in which a negative (often a double negative) is used to express a positive.

DEVELOPING YOUR IDEAS

2   Look at the description of the river. Decide which of these quotations is most important, and explain why.

- 'pulled herself up'
- 'spread her wings'
- 'bleeding through the camp'

- 'arming herself'
- 'ushered them off'

....

....

....

....

3   The poem begins with a very clear **exposition** of the story.

(a) Do you find the first line helpful or overly obvious?

....

(b) Which other poems in the collection use a similar technique in their opening lines?

....

....

Exposition: In narrative, this is where information is inserted to set out the plot or explain the scenario
being described.

TAKING IT FURTHER

4   One view is that this poem is unsatisfying because it treats the catastrophic events of the flood too lightly. On a separate piece of paper, write a paragraph arguing against this view, using at least five short quotations.

5   Compare the end of this poem with the final lines of 'Mametz Wood'. On a separate piece of paper, explain which you find more effective, and why.

Challenge yourself

Find out more about the village that inspired this poem, Dolwyddelan. In what ways is the description of the village here similar to or different from that of other Welsh landscapes you have encountered in your study of Sheers so far? What ideas might he be exploring in this poem that have not been explored in, for example, 'Y Gaer' or 'Skirrid Fawr'?

'History'

STARTING OUT

1   Circle the statement that is closer to your own views on this poem and explain your choice below.

● The poem is deceptively simple: beneath the monosyllabic lexis is a complex idea about how our social memory affects our identity.

● The poem is simple and effective: it directs the reader, leaving little room for thought, to do simple tasks and understand intuitively a simple way of life. It does not raise any challenging views or questions.

....

....

DEVELOPING YOUR IDEAS

2   Look at the second and third stanzas. The extended metaphor here is one of the bird's song being a chisel, although there are no sounds of industry in the valley any more. What is the effect of this image? How does it make you feel?

....

....

3   Does this remind you of another poem in the collection? Make brief notes on how they compare.

....

....

....

....

CONTINUED ➤

Answers can be found at: www.hoddereducation.co.uk/workbookanswers

4   Unusually for Sheers, the poem employs the imperative voice.

   (a) Highlight all the examples you can find in the poem.

   (b) What do you notice about the placement of these verbs in the poem? How are they placed within a line and within the whole text? Why might that be? On a separate piece of paper, write a PEA (Point/ Evidence/Analysis) paragraph in which you answer the question: What is the effect of the imperative voice in 'History'?

Imperative: Something that must be done or obeyed; an imperative verb demands action, such as 'Look' or 'Go'. Think about what kinds of texts use more of these verbs, and the effect they create.

TAKING IT FURTHER

5   The final lines are emphatic, using parallel syntax and visceral imagery to make clear Sheers' point. On a separate piece of paper, write a paragraph explaining his views.

'Amazon'*

STARTING OUT

1   (a) What connotations does the noun 'Amazon' have for you?

   ....

   (b) What does the adjective 'amazonian' mean?

   ....

2   One of the longest poems in the collection, 'Amazon' uses a straightforward chronological order to organise the text. However, there are both prolepsis and analepsis throughout. Label your text to show this, using arrows and labelling with how long a gap is being described in terms of minutes, hours, days and months.

Amazons: A mythical tribe of female warriors who cut off their right breast to aid in fighting. The myth may have been based on an ancient Iranian tribe.

Prolepsis: A jump forward in time.

Analepsis: A jump backwards in time.

Chronological: In time order.

Challenge yourself

Find out more about the Amazon tribe. Consider how else they or similar female characters are represented in literary or other forms of popular culture.

DEVELOPING YOUR IDEAS

3　How are sounds used in this poem? For each of the following quotations, explain the potential effects created.

   (a)　The sibilance of 'settling in her breast'

....

....

....

   (b)　The harsh sounds of 'can carry so much chaos'

....

....

....

   (c)　The plosive sounds in 'buses / redding past'

....

....

....

   (d)　The contrast in 'pop and smoky release'

....

....

....

4　One of the narrative features of this poem is its use of adverbs. For each of the following examples, comment on the effect created and how it shapes our view of the woman at the centre of the story.

   (a)　'idly'

....

....

   (b)　'kindly'

....

....

....

CONTINUED ➡

　　　　　Answers can be found at: www.hoddereducation.co.uk/workbookanswers

(c) 'quietly'

....

....

....

(d) 'mostly'

....

....

....

TAKING IT FURTHER

5 The poem ends with a notable and solitary line, reflecting the woman's independence and confidence. Annotate around the line to explore all the connotations and ideas you can think of. Start with the underlined key words, then consider sound and syntax.

'able to draw her bow <u>further and deeper</u> than other women.'

6 Sheers tends to describe experiences from a masculine perspective, even if the plot is about a couple. How convincing do you find his description of this very vulnerable and feminine experience? On a separate piece of paper, write an extended response in which you explore at least ten quotations from this poem and three from other poems in the collection by way of comparison.

KEY SKILLS

Exploring ambiguity will help you to access the top grades: try to find at least one line in each poem that has more than one interpretation. It may be useful to use the two adverbs 'literally' and metaphorically' as a starting point.

Practice examination essay

The previous four poems ('Four Movements', 'Liable to Floods', 'History' and 'Amazon') have offered a range of different ideas about the past and its impact. Using these poems as the basis for your answer, use the structured plan below to formulate an answer to the exam-style question:

'In *Skirrid Hill* the past is revelatory rather than painful.'

How far do you agree with this view?

STARTING OUT

Introduction

1 (a) Define terms: 'Revelatory' means … **(AO1: clarity, shaped response)**

....

....

....

(b) Contemporary literature tends to avoid religious ideas when discussing revelations, and instead focuses on … **(AO4: typicality)**

....

....

(c) In most twentieth-century literature, revelation and identity are depicted as … **(AO4: typicality)**

....

....

DEVELOPING YOUR IDEAS

2 (a) Find quotations and give a brief analysis of each quotation to support the idea that: The past is revelatory rather than painful.

....

....

....

....

(b) Pivotal moments are depicted as moments of clarity in Sheers' work. **(AO2: analysis of language, structure and form)**

....

....

....

....

....

CONTINUED ➡

(c) Longer spans of time, such as medical treatment or wars, are also didactic experiences for Sheers. **(AO2: analysis of language, structure and form)**

....

....

....

....

(d) Find quotations and give a brief analysis of each quotation to support the idea that the past is painful rather than revelatory.

....

....

....

....

(e) No, Sheers implies that society's past is painful and we do not learn from it. **(Include some AO3: social and historical context here, such as the Second World War)**

....

....

....

....

....

TAKING IT FURTHER

Conclusion

3 Find quotations and give a brief analysis of each quotation to support the idea the following idea: **(AO5: debate)** Sheers also suggests that, although we may learn from the past, it was painful and problematic at the time.

....

....

....

....

....

'Shadow Man'

STARTING OUT

1   Which other poems are dedicated to a person and to whom are they dedicated?

....

....

2   Are there any similarities between the dedicatees of these poems?

....

....

DEVELOPING YOUR IDEAS

3   Read more about the artist on his website (search for 'Mac Adams') and look at the images of his work. Note the titles and postmodern qualities of his work. On a separate piece of paper, make notes on any links you can make between his work and that of Sheers.

4   Although the poem seems simple, describing how Mac Adams uses unlikely objects to create shadow images, there are some more philosophical and complex ideas hidden within a relatively straightforward lexis. For each of the suggested effects, select an appropriate quotation for evidence.

POSSIBLE EFFECTS CREATED	QUOTATION
The artist is seen as a mysterious and complex character, with almost omnipotent qualities.	
Sheers creates an unsettling mood of bathos by contrasting a significant figure with the objects used to create the image.	
Sheers tries to focus the reader's attention on the specific, revelatory moment of seeing something fleeting as a way of reiterating one of the key themes of the collection: that pivotal moments affect our whole lives and ways of thinking.	

TAKING IT FURTHER

5   Which other poems are about moments of revelation or inspiration? Write down the five most important below.

....

....

....

6   The poem ends with Sheers' message. Sum this up in one sentence.

....

....

7   The use of the noun 'shadows' at the end is ambiguous and cryptic. If shadows usually connote death and threat, is there another way of reading this poem other than your answer in Question 6?

....

....

Challenge yourself

The poet and critic W.H. Auden once described all geniuses as being somewhat suspicious or 'shady'. Considering the artists and writers you listed in Question 1, do you think Sheers would agree with this statement?

'Under the Superstition Mountains'

STARTING OUT

The epigraph comes from song 'Susan's House' by a 1990s band called Eels. Watch the video on YouTube.

1   Why has the epigraph been chosen? What do you notice about the pace and style of the music?

....

....

2   Look at the quotation: 'hiding behind this picket fence'. What places, times and ideas does a picket fence usually connote?

....

....

DEVELOPING YOUR IDEAS

3   For each of the themes below, list as many short quotations as you can find in the poem. Some may be appropriate in more than one box.

NATURE	DEATH
CULTURE	**TECHNOLOGY**

4   The poem uses a number of potentially ambiguous images to evoke the unsettling atmosphere of Sun City West, a suburb inhabited only by those aged over 65. For each of the following quotations, list two possible interpretations.

(a) 'keep check on each others' houses' ....

....

....

(b) 'sedated by the heat' ....

....

....

(c) 'without knowing why' ....

....

....

TAKING IT FURTHER

5   The poem's depiction of the final decades of life is predominately described with a tone of disbelief and distance. Compare this poem with others on a similar topic. Which do you find more convincing, and why? Make notes below.

(a)   'Trees'

....

....

....

CONTINUED ➡

(b) 'On Going'

....

....

....

(c) 'The Wake'

....

....

....

6 If you are taking the WJEC or Eduqas exam, make notes on a separate piece of paper, comparing Sheers with Heaney's poems. Make sure you use lots of key quotations from both texts.

'Service'

STARTING OUT

1 Look at the list of occupations mentioned in the poem.

| 'chippy' | 'Sommelier' | 'Matador' | 'boxer' |

| 'chef' | 'graduate' | 'army recruit' |

| 'jockey' | 'waiter' | 'Suit' |

| 'author' | 'father' | 'son' |

(a) Look up and make a note of the definitions of any you did not already know.

(b) Highlight any that have been mentioned in other poems in the collection and make of a note of the poems in which they appeared.

(c) In one colour circle the five that you think are most 'masculine'.

(d) In another colour, circle the five that you think Sheers most admires, from the way he describes them.

2 The poem goes through many subtle shifts in tone.

(a) For each adjective, find evidence from the text. (To help you, these are in order from start to finish.)

Contemplative	
Bustling	
Practised	

CONTINUED ➡

Mysterious	
Plentiful	
Frantic	
Ponderous	
Quiet	

DEVELOPING YOUR IDEAS

Parts of the poem are delivered by an intrusive narrator, almost like a chorus in a tragedy. Note how this voice is not omniscient (all knowing) as it asks questions, as well as providing a commentary and directing the attention of the reader. In many ways, the poem is more like a documentary film or performance than a poem.

3   For each of the quotations below and on the following page, explain the effects created. Use some of the suggested vocabulary below to help in your answers.

authoritative   clichéd   didactic   direct   metaphorical   performative

playful   polysyndeton   rhetorical   self-conscious   sparse

Didactic: Teaching or telling.

Polysyndeton: The use of repeated link words, such as 'and'.

(a) 'Imagine a theatre' ....

....

(b) 'This is what it's like' ....

....

(c) 'Behind this a witch's cauldron' ....

....

(d) 'And so it goes' ....

....

(e) '12.45 - the first cover is in' ....

....

CONTINUED ➔

(f) 'So, what's the story here?' ....

....

(g) 'And the stories go the other way too' ....

....

4 Sheers' choice of which food to describe is interesting: the restaurant he observed to write this poem is famous for unusual ingredients and innovative methods. Make brief notes in the spaces below on the foods and methods he describes and the possible reasons for those choices.

FOODSTUFFS	METHODS
POSSIBLE REASONS OR IMPLICATIONS?	**POSSIBLE REASONS OR IMPLICATIONS?**

5 The poem is punctuated by individual lines. Put these in order by numbering them, and annotate each one to suggest the effect created.

'Check!'	
'Done! You can go on that one!'	
'Four oysters away!'	
'How long on the chicken?'	
'And so it goes'	
'Radio off'	

CONTINUED ➡

'So, what's the story here?'	
'This is what it's like'	

TAKING IT FURTHER

6   The poem ends with a return to the character of the Sommelier from the opening stanzas. On a separate piece of paper, write a paragraph in which you explore the way in which he and other men in the poem are presented. Is this typical of Sheers' ideas about men and labour? Refer to at least two other poems from the collection in your answer.

7   The poem is reminiscent of Seamus Heaney's 'Oysters'. Find the poem online and compare its first two stanzas with the section of Sheers' 'Service' on the same topic. On a separate piece of paper, make brief notes on how they differ in terms of emotion and perspective.

Challenge yourself

The poem was written while Sheers was poet-in-residence at the famous restaurant The Fat Duck in Bray, owned by innovative chef Heston Blumenthal. Sheers wrote 'Hedge School' during the same period. What similarities can you see between the two poems in terms of style or content?

'The Fishmonger'

STARTING OUT

1   Sum up each of the six tercets with one abstract noun or emotion.

(a) ....

(b) ....

(c) ....

(d) ....

(e) ....

(f) ....

DEVELOPING YOUR IDEAS

2   Note the use of **zeugma** in the pivotal line 'how to pare his speech as he might men'. How does this change our feelings about the fishmonger, and about the poem?

....

....

....

....

....

....

Zeugma: Applying one verb to two different things.

3   Why is the phrase 'understanding as only he can' repeated? Think of at least two potential explanations.

....

....

....

....

4   The poem has a menacing undertone. Choose the five most effective phrases from the poem to explain this.

....

....

....

5   The fishmonger can be seen as more sympathetic and misunderstood, however. On a separate piece of paper, write a paragraph that expands on this idea, using the quotations provided.

- 'unsteady'
- 'ingrown nail'
- 'understanding as only he can'
- 'were he hurt and pushed'
- 'no healing bark'
- 'gasps for growth'

TAKING IT FURTHER

6   Look at:
- another English poet's translation (search for 'Antony Dunn Fishmonger')
- a further translation in the online answers to this revision book.

Compare these with Sheers' version. Each is subtly different in terms of structure, focus and mood. Which do you prefer and why? On a separate piece of paper, make brief notes on each.

7   Which stanza is most important in conveying the character of the fishmonger, in your opinion? On a separate piece of paper, write a paragraph in which you argue your case.

'Stitch in Time'

STARTING OUT

1 (a) What is the full idiom from which the title is taken?

....

....

(b) What does it imply?

....

....

(c) How does this relate to the plot and message of the poem?

....

....

....

....

> **Idiom**: Everyday saying where the literal meaning does not convey what is implied: for example, raining cats and dogs.

DEVELOPING YOUR IDEAS

2 For each of the points below, provide a quotation from the poem as evidence, explain the effect created and make a link to another poem from the collection that uses the same technique.

POINT	Beginning the poem by implying this is part of a larger conversation	Musical imagery to describe the human form	Bird imagery
EVIDENCE			
EFFECT			
LINK TO ANOTHER POEM			

CONTINUED ➡

Answers can be found at: www.hoddereducation.co.uk/workbookanswers

3   On a copy of the poem, use one colour to highlight masculine rhymes and another colour for feminine rhymes. On a separate piece of paper, make notes on where each is used, and on which couplets do not rhyme, and what this might suggest.

Masculine rhyme: Where the final rhymed syllables are stressed, like *blow/go*.

Feminine rhyme: A rhyme of two syllables (of which the second is unstressed) or of three syllables (of which the second and third are unstressed), for example *motion/ocean* or *glamorous/amorous*.

Couplet: A pair of successsive lines of verse.

4   The poem focuses predominately on the protagonist's actions. For each action, suggest what personal qualities are connoted by what he does.

(a)   Travels back ....

   ....

(b)   Tailors suits ....

   ....

(c)   Returns for his wife ....

   ....

(d)   Visits London ....

   ....

TAKING IT FURTHER

'This poem encompasses all the major themes of the collection: masculinity and work, pivotal moments in life, relationships, and identity in the modern world. It is the key to the whole collection.'

How far do you agree with this statement?

5   Write an essay plan for the above question, using the sub-questions below to help structure your argument:

(a)   Do you agree these are the main themes? What else would you add?

   ....

   ....

   ....

   ....

(b)   Which other poems are especially important to the collection? Why?

   ....

   ....

   ....

   ....

CONTINUED ➜

(c) Is the poem as memorable and effective as others in the collection? What were your first thoughts on reading it?

....

....

....

....

....

(d) Continuing on a separate piece of paper, plan your answer under the following headings:

- Yes – reasons to agree
- No – reasons to disagree
- However …

'L.A. Evening'

STARTING OUT

1 Look up definitions for each of the following feelings:

(a) Ennui ....

(b) Nostalgia ....

(c) Melancholy ....

(d) Poignancy ....

(e) Sadness ....

(f) Loneliness ....

2 Which word from Question 1 do you think best fits the poem? On a separate piece of paper, write a paragraph justifying your choice, using at least three short quotations from the poem.

3 Who do you think the woman is? Use the online answers to find out, then research her life and make notes on a separate piece of paper.

4 What effect is created by the anonymity Sheers uses here? Try to think of at least three reasons.

- ....

....

- ....

....

- ....

....

DEVELOPING YOUR IDEAS

5   Choose quotations from the poem as evidence of the ideas below:

The first stanza shows how all action takes place outside the subject's house, exacerbating her feelings of isolation and stasis.	
The second stanza refers to great moments in cinema to contrast the poignancy of the first stanza, and to explain briefly the woman's achievements.	
The third stanza uses sinister sounds and images to reflect the melancholy feeling and setting.	
The fourth stanza is not pitiable, but evokes feelings of resignation and ennui.	

TAKING IT FURTHER

'Sheers' depiction of ageing in the collection is more thoughtful and reverent than his depiction of youth.'
Examine this view of Sheer's presentation of age in the collection.

6   Write an essay plan for the above question, using the sub-questions below to help structure your argument. Write your plan on a separate piece of paper.

   (a) How would you characterise his depiction of ageing? Which poems are most useful for this?

   (b) How would you characterise his depiction of youth? Which poems are most useful for this?

   (c) Continuing on a separate piece of paper, plan your answer under the following headings:

   - Yes – reasons to agree
   - No – reasons to disagree
   - However ...

Challenge yourself

'All writers, all artists of any kind, in so far as they have had any philosophical or critical power, perhaps just in so far as they have been deliberate artists at all, have had some philosophy, some criticism of their art: and it has often been this philosophy [...] that has evoked their most startling inspiration.'

William Butler Yeats, 'The Symbolism of Poetry' (1900)

Sheers often uses ideas about other forms of culture – photography, music, writing, drama and performance, visual art, cinema – in his work. What does this suggest about his feelings towards poetry, and towards those different forms?

'The Singing Men'*

STARTING OUT

1   Circle the statement that comes closer to encapsulating your view of the poem and explain your choice in the space below.

  ● The poem exudes a sense of pathos at the men's reduced circumstances and applauds their determination to sing despite their difficulties.

  ● The poem is an unsettling celebration of potentially aggressive characters and undesirable by-products of modern urban life.

....

....

....

....

....

....

....

....

DEVELOPING YOUR IDEAS

2   What do the following two terms mean? Find a definition, and then use each in a sentence about the poem.

  (a) Deracinate

   ....

   ....

  (b) Liminal

   ....

   ....

CONTINUED

Answers can be found at: www.hoddereducation.co.uk/workbookanswers

3 For each of the following key quotations, explain the effects created. Try to think of two meanings or ideas for each, using as guidance the two opposing views in Question 1.

(a) 'singing for their supper or just for the hell of it'

....

....

(b) 'but had lives, in which, if they were lucky'

....

....

(c) 'the world's greatest group'

....

....

(d) 'legs open, welcoming the commuters home'

....

....

TAKING IT FURTHER

4 On a separate piece of paper, list arguments and quotations to support and to oppose the following view, with reference to 'The Singing Men' and related poems in the collection.

'In *Skirrid Hill*, masculinity is presented as power rather than emotional depth, characterised by action not thought.'

5 (a) Then write a paragraph outlining the view you find less convincing. Begin your paragraph 'A less convincing view is that ...'

(b) Then write a paragraph outlining the view you find more convincing. Begin your paragraph 'Rather more convincing is the view that ...'

KEY SKILLS

Comparing texts requires a wide range of vocabulary. Quantifiers such as **most** or **least** can be useful, as can linking words like **whereas**. List as many comparing words and phrases as you can in the space below.

....

....

....

....

Challenge yourself

What roles do singers and storytellers have in modern life and/or literature through the ages? List as many examples as you can.

'The Wake'*

STARTING OUT

1 On a copy of the poem, highlight in one colour words to do with the body, and in another colour words related to ships or the sea. What do you notice about their frequency and placement?

....

....

....

....

2 The word 'wake' (noun or verb) has many different meanings. For each potential implication below, suggest how this is relevant to the poem. Write your answers on a separate piece of paper.

(a) To be awakened

(b) The gathering after a funeral

(c) The ripples after a ship has passed

DEVELOPING YOUR IDEAS

3 From the words that you highlighted in Question 1, choose the three most important examples related to each idea below and explain the effects created.

	THE BODY	SHIPS OR THE SEA
A		
B		
C		

CONTINUED

Answers can be found at: www.hoddereducation.co.uk/workbookanswers

4   Although some stanzas are joined together with enjambment, the poem's structure is made clear through the first, fifth and final two stanzas. For each, make brief notes on the tone and most important phrases.

STANZAS	TONE	KEY QUOTATIONS AND IDEAS
1		
5		
9 and 10		

TAKING IT FURTHER

5   What is the effect of omitting the speech that passes between the two characters?

....

....

....

....

6   Which poem do you find more moving: 'The Wake', 'On Going', or 'Y Gaer'/'Hill Fort'? On a separate piece of paper, explain your views in an extended response that quotes from each of these poems, and that considers structure, sound and imagery.

Challenge yourself

'What are the eternal objects of poetry, among all nations and at all times? They are actions; human actions; possessing an inherent interest in themselves, and which are to be communicated in an interesting manner by the art of the poet. [...] The poet, then, has in the first place to select an excellent action; and **what actions are most excellent?** Those, certainly, which most powerfully appeal to the great human primary affections: to **those elementary feelings** which subsist permanently in the race, and are independent of time.'

Matthew Arnold: Preface to 'The Poems of Matthew Arnold' (1853) [my emphasis]

Matthew Arnold was a famous Victorian poet and critic, who argues that great poetry must be about universal and important experiences. How convincing do you find this view, and how could you use Sheers' poem 'The Wake' to defend your ideas?

'Skirrid Fawr'*

STARTING OUT

1   With what do we associate hills and mountains? Add your ideas to the diagram below.

Hills and mountains

powerful and looming

legends/myths

wildlife

DEVELOPING YOUR IDEAS

2   The poem acts as a kind of epilogue, a homecoming where Sheers can revisit the same landscape and reflect on his own development and life. Explain the effect created by each quotation below, and then rank them (from 1 for the most important to 5 for the least important).

QUOTATION	EFFECT	RANK
'I am still drawn to her back for the answers'		
'the split view she reveals'		
'a lonely hulk'		

CONTINUED ➔

QUOTATION	EFFECT	RANK
'unspoken words'		
'unlearned tongue'		

TAKING IT FURTHER

'[Poetry should be] fitting to metrical arrangement a selection of the real language of men in a state of vivid sensation.'

William Wordsworth, Preface to *Lyrical Ballads, with Pastoral and other Poems (1802): The Subject and Language of Poetry*

How far is this statement true of 'Skirrid Fawr' and the collection as a whole?

3 (a) Write an essay plan for this question. Complete the sub-questions below to help you structure your argument.

(i) How accessible and effective is the collection in terms of language (consider colloquialisms, idiom, vernacular, dialect, Welsh/English, etc.)?

(ii) How far are Sheers' poems 'vivid'? Which did you find most memorable? Visual? Interesting? Relevant?

(iii) Continuing on a separate piece of paper, plan your answer under the following headings:
- Yes – reasons to agree
- No – reasons to disagree
- However …

(b) When you have finished planning, write a full essay. If you are taking the WJEC or Eduqas exam, write a section on Sheers and then a section on Heaney, and compare them in a conclusion.

Challenge yourself
Reviewing the poems
- Can you remember the names of all 42 poems? Try to list them from memory.
- Now draw four boxes and label the first one 'Most Welsh', the second 'Most intimate and personal', the third 'Most general and social' and the last one 'Most international'. Place each poem in one of the boxes. A poem may go in more than one box.

Boosting your skills

STARTING OUT

Understanding the Assessment Objectives

1   In your exam you will be marked according to five Assessment Objectives (AOs), which are the same for both AS- and A-level These are shown below. Under each AO, add your own examples of what each might mean or include. The first has been done for you.

> AO1: Articulate informed, personal and creative responses to literary texts, using associated concepts and terminology, and coherent, accurate written expression.
>
> *My own ideas, using technical English words with no spelling or grammar errors.*

> AO2: Analyse ways in which meanings are shaped in literary texts.
>
> ....
>
> ....

> AO3: Demonstrate understanding of the significance and influence of the contexts in which literary texts are written and received.
>
> ....
>
> ....

> AO4: Explore connections across literary texts.
>
> ....
>
> ....

> AO5: Explore literary texts informed by different interpretations.
>
> ....
>
> ....

DEVELOPING YOUR IDEAS

Preparing to answer the question (AO1)

Sometimes the Assessment Objectives are asking you to take what you were doing previously at GCSE to a higher level. You will be familiar already with shaping your personal interpretation into a coherent answer to the essay question; using appropriate subject-related terminology; analysing the form, structure and language of texts; and drawing upon context.

At AS/A-level there is greater emphasis under AO1 on the quality of your own essay writing, and your ability to shape your points into a coherent line of argument. Candidates sometimes separate out the Assessment Objectives with a line in each paragraph on each AO, but you should avoid this. The Assessment Objectives should be blended together in a holistic way. You might, for example, when discussing language, consider how a particular word may have different connotations for its contemporary audience from those it has for

CONTINUED

a feminist reader. Don't just tag on a critic's opinion: instead build it into your own response to the ideas, language and form within context, stating where you agree with the critic, and where you disagree.

The first thing you should do when faced with the examination question is to take a deep breath! That achieved, read the question carefully, and annotate it, underlining each of the following:

- Actions and verbs
- Names of any critics or specified poems
- The main idea, which you are being asked to debate and evaluate

Then jot down the poems that immediately spring to mind (from Heaney as well as Sheers if you are taking the WJEC or Eduqas exams).

2 Practise by writing each of these statements on to a separate piece of paper, annotating them and then making preliminary notes on how you might answer the question: How far do you agree? Use the headings 'reason to agree' and 'reasons to disagree' to help you.

   (a) **'Masculinity is always powerful and destructive in the poems.' Examine this view.**

   (b) **'Relationships are always damaged and unsuccessful in the poems.' How far do you agree?**

   (c) **'Pivotal moments are more significant than longer spans of time in the poems.' Examine this view.**

3 Now, on a separate piece of paper, begin to plan your essay: you can choose any of the three statements given in Question 2.

   Start to think about the order in which you wish to present your ideas. Add numbers or arrows on your planning page to show which ideas could flow smoothly onto the next. Don't be afraid to cross out less effective points or ideas, which will help you keep momentum and focus on your best points as you write.

4 Now sketch out your refined essay plan, complete with terminology, context and verbs. Aim to have roughly half your points agreeing with the statement, and half disagreeing.

Constructing an argument and writing effectively (AO1)

Your introduction should include your argument that you intend to pursue, some **historical references**, a brief discussion of how **typical** Sheers' approach is of post-1945 poetry in your view, and one sentence on what an **opposing argument** might suggest.

5 Colour code each of the bold words in this instruction, and then use these colours to highlight the student example below.

Owen Sheers says the word 'Skirrid' is derived from a Welsh word meaning 'divorce or separation'.

Examine the view that the collection is characterised by the theme of separation

> It could be argued that 'Skirrid Hill' is a collection
>
> characterised by the theme of separation. Separation is
>
> an idea typical to modernist poetry, and is the action of
>
> something being moved apart, and the division of something
>
> being disconnected and detached. This links closely to the
>
> theme of divorce, a word that Owen Sheers says 'Skirrid' can
>
> translate as. Divorce is the separation between things

CONTINUED ➤

which ought to be connected. Separation is something

that runs through most if not all the poems, with it being

especially prominent in the poems 'Border Country' and

'Keyways'. However, it could be argued that the poems are

more characterised by the theme of performance, a typical

postmodern theme, something that is explored in the

poem 'Winter Swans'. It seems though that ultimately the

poems are more adequately characterised by the theme of

separation, as even that can be found in 'Winter Swans', and it

runs as an undercurrent seemingly subconsciously to most

if not all of Sheers poetry.

6   Annotate the example with changes you could make or terms you could add to improve it.

Using textual references

Even if your exam board allows you a copy of the text in the exam itself, hunting for references is not a good use of your exam time. You need to know the poems extremely well.

Quotations should be written exactly as they are in the original text, including capitals letters and any punctuation: a comma can significantly change the meaning of the line, so copy carefully when making your notes. Although your references should be very short and precise, they could well be from enjambed lines of stanzas. In this case, don't forget the conventions of punctuation.

Look at 'Swallows' again. To quote words across two lines, you should use an oblique or forward slash, as shown below. Note the capital letters and absence of them, too.

'italic again, / cutting'

To quote words across two stanzas, you should use two obliques.

'crossed crossed lines. // Their annual regeneration'

Again, notice how the punctuation of the original has been retained, such as the full stop.

7   For each poem, take one A4 sheet of paper, and write on it the **ten most important quotations** of **three words or fewer.** Then annotate each quotation with terminology, the main effect created by it, and typicality comments. Look for ambiguity and different views, too. The example below shows how might start. You might like to decorate your diagrams with images, drawn or printed, to make them more memorable.

CONTINUED

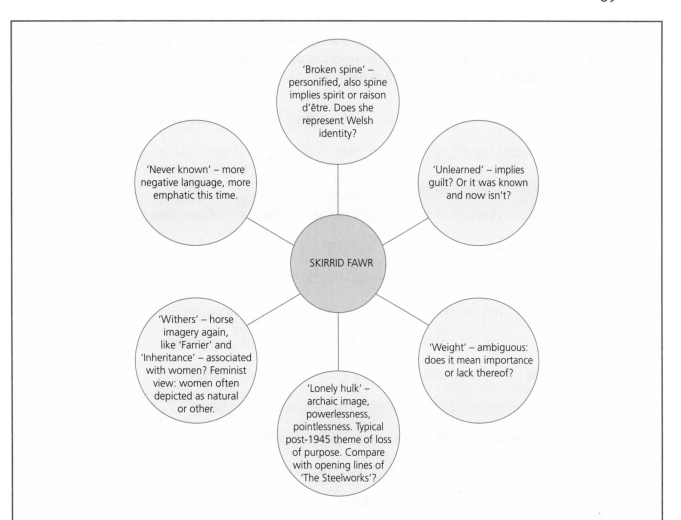

Analysing language, structure and form, and exploring the ways meanings are shaped (AO2)

When you are thinking about AO2, you are focusing not just on what the poet has to say, but on how they have chosen to express these ideas. This will not only mean looking in detail at language and structure, but also thinking about form and genre. Remember that AO2 asks you to explore ways in which **meanings** are **shaped**. This means your focus should be on how the poet conveys meaning using literary techniques – not on poetic techniques in isolation.

8   You will need to have a wide critical vocabulary. In the table below, list as many terms as you can that relate to each area. Why not try doing this against a stopwatch for ten minutes?

Language and imagery	Sound	Structure and time
Parts of speech	Writers and characters	Punctuation and pauses

Check your answers against the online answers for this book. Make flashcards of terms and their meanings for any you don't already use habitually, and use them to revise.

CONTINUED ➡

9   Read this exemplar paragraph. Annotate it to show which words and ideas are effective and which are less so. Give this a mark out of 25, and write a brief report as an examiner will when they finish reading your essay. How well does it meet AO1 and AO5 in particular?

> In 'The Farrier' Sheers begins the collection with immediate
> respect for physical labour. Images of 'man putting his shoulder
> against a knackered car' epitomise masculine tendencies,
> portraying a clear archetypal image. The reader notices how
> he smokes a 'roll up' which suggests a kind of traditional
> masculinity and a timeless quality to the character in the
> poem. The more shocking image in the poem of him giving
> the horse 'a slap' implies a lack of respect, and, given that
> the horse has been described in feminine terms, suggests
> a problematic attitude towards women which modern
> readers are likely to find distasteful. The tone of the poem
> here becomes domineering, having changed from an initial
> appreciation of manual work.

10   What could you add to improve it? Annotate in a different colour, adding terms, quotations and ideas.

Using context (AO3)

11   On a separate piece of paper, draw a timeline that extends from 1900 at the top of the page to the present day at the bottom. Add dates at 25-year intervals. Then plot on your timeline major events of relevance, such as world wars, to the left of the line, and any historical or literary events or people mentioned in the collection, such as the rule of 'Hitler' Hunzvi, closure of 'Ebbw Vale, 'Mametz Wood', to the right of the line. If you are comparing Sheers to Heaney, write those relevant to Sheers in one colour, to Heaney in another, and to both in a third colour. Highlight the most important and make a more detailed revision flashcard on them to add to those you have already made on the poems.

TAKING IT FURTHER

Exploring connections across texts (AO4)

12   War and other forms of conflict form a central theme of this collection.

Sheers has written a novel about the Second World War, called *Resistance*, as well as plays about soldiers wounded in more recent conflicts: *The Two Worlds of Charlie F* and *Pink Mist*.

Which poems are explicitly about war and its aftermath? Record the titles here and make notes on any significant similarities in the voice, style, tone or message.

....

....

CONTINUED ➡

....

....

....

13 Social change and Welsh identity is another key theme in the collection. Lisa Gee said that 'Sheers's poems are imbued with a deep love of, and feeling for, Wales.'

Which poems are explicitly about Welsh identity and social change since 1945? Record the titles here and make notes on any significant similarities in the voice, style, tone or message.

....

....

....

....

14 Sarah Crown argues that the dominant theme of the collection is landscape and separation.

Which poems are explicitly about landscape and place? Record the titles here and make notes on any significant similarities in the voice, style, tone or message. Decide whether you agree with Sarah Crown.

....

....

....

....

15 Love, romance and sex are key themes in the collection. In an earlier poem, Sheers referred to 'the persistence of love', and his writing in *Skirrid Hill* is sometimes described as 'sensuous'. Some would argue that this is the dominant theme of the collection.

Which poems are explicitly about love, sex or romance? Record the titles here and make notes on any significant similarities in the voice, style, tone or message. Decide whether you agree with the above argument.

....

....

....

....

....

....

CONTINUED ➤

Essay planning and different interpretations (AO5)

16 Use a stopwatch for this activity. For each of the suggested essay titles below, do the following:

(a) 'Relationships are always artificial and unsuccessful performances in *Skirrid Hill*.' How far do you agree?

(b) 'Physical labour is essential to masculinity and identity in Sheers' work.' How far do you agree?

(c) 'Memories always damage the present in *Skirrid Hill*.' How far do you agree?

For the first ten minutes, **jot down your ideas** under the following headings, **without looking at the text**:

- Evidence for
- Context and typicality points to support this view
- Evidence against
- Context and typicality points to support this view
- Your answer, in one sentence
- For the next ten minutes, open the collection and **find precise quotations** from three or four poems.
- For the next ten minutes, **draft an introduction** – using the notes you have made.

Answers can be found on: www.hoddereducation.co.uk/workbookanswers

The Publishers would like to thank the following for permission to reproduce copyright material.

Throughout: Owen Sheers: from *Skirrid Hill* (Seren Books, 2005), copyright © Owen Sheers, reproduced by permission of the author c/o Rogers, Coleridge & White Ltd., 20 Powis Mews, London W11 1JN; **p.26, 48, 53 and 106; Sarah Crown:** from 'Parting of the ways (and other dislocations)' (*Guardian*, 25 February 2006), © Guardian News and Media 2018; **p.43, 106: Lisa Gee:** from 'Owen Sheers: The blue-eyed boy and bard' (*Independent*, 9 December 2005), reproduced with permission of Independent Digital News & Media Ltd.

Every effort has been made to trace all copyright holders, but if any have been inadvertently overlooked, the Publishers will be pleased to make the necessary arrangements at the first opportunity.

Although every effort has been made to ensure that website addresses are correct at time of going to press, Hodder Education cannot be held responsible for the content of any website mentioned in this book. It is sometimes possible to find a relocated web page by typing in the address of the home page for a website in the URL window of your browser.

Hachette UK's policy is to use papers that are natural, renewable and recyclable products and made from wood grown in sustainable forests. The logging and manufacturing processes are expected to conform to the environmental regulations of the country of origin.

Orders: please contact Bookpoint Ltd, 130 Park Drive, Milton Park, Abingdon, Oxon OX14 4SE. Telephone: (44) 01235 827720. Fax: (44) 01235 400401. Email education@bookpoint.co.uk Lines are open from 9 a.m. to 5 p.m., Monday to Saturday, with a 24-hour message answering service. You can also order through our website: www.hoddereducation.co.uk

ISBN: 978 1 5104 3496 7

© Helen Mars 2018

First published in 2018 by
Hodder Education,
An Hachette UK Company
Carmelite House
50 Victoria Embankment
London EC4Y 0DZ

www.hoddereducation.co.uk

Impression number   10 9 8 7 6 5 4 3 2 1

Year   2021 2020 2019 2018

All rights reserved. Apart from any use permitted under UK copyright law, no part of this publication may be reproduced or transmitted in any form or by any means, electronic or mechanical, including photocopying and recording, or held within any information storage and retrieval system, without permission in writing from the publisher or under licence from the Copyright Licensing Agency Limited. Further details of such licences (for reprographic reproduction) may be obtained from the Copyright Licensing Agency Limited, www.cla.co.uk

Cover photo © PsychoShadowMaker/iStock/Thinkstock/Getty Images

Illustrations by Integra Software Services Pvt. Ltd.

Typeset in Integra Software Services Pvt. Ltd., Pondicherry, India

Printed in Spain

A catalogue record for this title is available from the British Library.

HODDER EDUCATION

t: 01235 827827
e: education@bookpoint.co.uk
w: hoddereducation.co.uk

ISBN 978-1-5104-3496-7

9 781510 434967

MIX
Paper from
responsible sources
FSC™ C104740